Taking Care of Our World

Thelma Rea

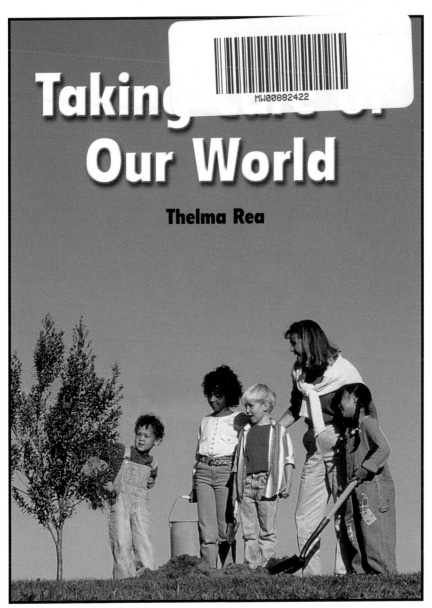

Rosen REAL READERS

Rosen Classroom Books & Materials
New York

In our world we need clean air to **breathe**. We also need clean water to drink.

In our world we need clean and safe places to live and play.

You can do something every day
to help take care of our land,
water, and air.

You can put **trash** in trash cans to help keep our parks and playgrounds clean.

You can pick up trash on our beaches to help keep them clean.

You can save used **bottles** and cans. They will be used again to make new ones.

You can use something more
than one time before you throw
it away.

You can walk to the store instead
of driving a car. This helps keep
our air clean.

You can help plant a tree. Trees help keep our air and water clean.

How will you help take care of our world today?

Glossary

bottle   Something used to hold drinks and other things that are like water.

breathe   To take air into your body through your nose or mouth and then send it back out.

trash   Things that are not needed and can be thrown away.